NASA

NASA

USA

SPACE SHUTTLE

SPACE SHUTTLE

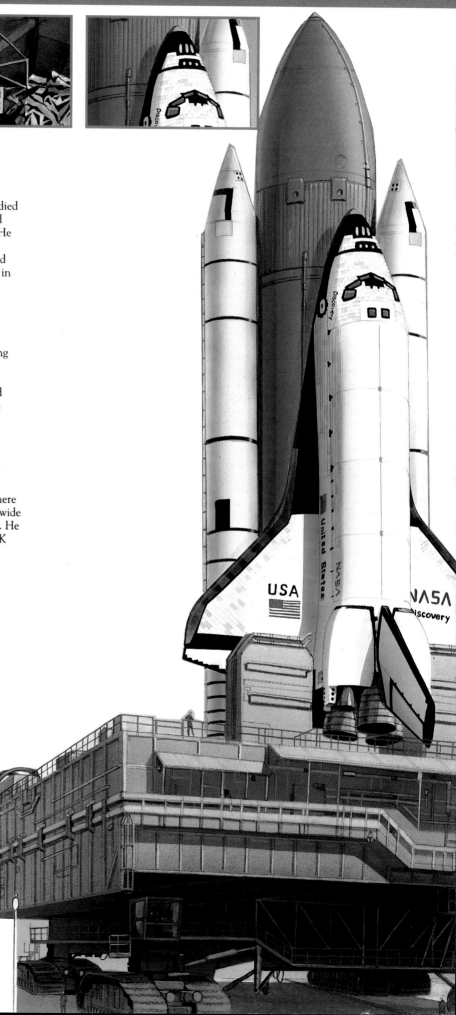

Editor   Penny Clarke

Artist and Author:

Mark Bergin was born in Hastings in 1961. He studied at Eastbourne College of Art and has specialized in historical reconstructions, aviation and maritime subjects since 1983. He has been commissioned by aerospace companies and has illustrated a number of books on flight. He has also illustrated many books in the prize-winning *Inside Story* series. He lives in Bexhill-on-Sea, England, with his wife and three children.

Consultant:

Peter Turvey is a Project Manager at the Science Museum, London. He has worked on many projects, including the Telecommunications, Space and Challenge of Materials galleries, as well as on the construction of a Victorian 'calculating engine' designed by Charles Babbage. He studied physics and astronomy at the University of Leicester and the History of Technology at Imperial College, London. He has written **Inventions** in the *Timelines* series and **The X-Ray Picture Book of Everyday Things**.

Series creator:

David Salariya was born in Dundee, Scotland, where he studied illustration and printmaking. He has illustrated a wide range of books on botanical, historical and mythical subjects. He has created many new series of books for publishers in the UK and overseas. In 1989 he established The Salariya Book Company. He lives in Brighton, England, with his wife, the illustrator Shirley Willis, and their son Jonathan.

Created, designed and produced by
THE SALARIYA BOOK COMPANY LTD
25 Marlborough Place, Brighton BN1 1UB

ISBN 0-531-14573-5 (Lib. Bdg.)
     0-531-15423-8 (Pbk.)

First American Edition 1999 by
Franklin Watts
Grolier Publishing Co., Inc.
Sherman Turnpike
Danbury, CT 06816

Visit Franklin Watts on the Internet at:
http://publishing.grolier.com

A catalog record for this title is available from the Library of Congress.

Printed in Singapore.

SPACE
SHUTTLE

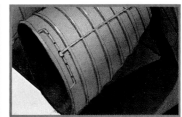

Written and illustrated by

MARK BERGIN

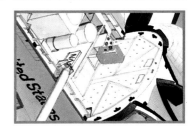

Created and designed by

DAVID SALARIYA

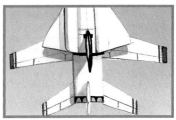

W
FRANKLIN WATTS
A Division of Grolier Publishing
NEW YORK • LONDON • HONG KONG • SYDNEY
DANBURY, CONNECTICUT

Contents

The Space Race

In the early 1960s the United States (U.S.) and the Soviet Union (U.S.S.R.) were hostile to each other. On April 12, 1961, the U.S.S.R. sent cosmonaut (the Russian word for astronaut) Yuri Gagarin into space. Then, on May 25, President Kennedy promised that the U.S. would land a man on the moon by 1970. The space race between the U.S. and the U.S.S.R. had started. The National Aeronautics and Space Administration (NASA) began the Apollo program to meet the challenge.

For the next few years both nations sent many unmanned spacecraft to the moon. Then, on July 20, 1969, American astronaut Neil Armstrong set foot on the moon and uttered the words "That's one small step for man, one giant leap for mankind." The U.S. had won the space race.

The landing site was called Tranquillity Base. Astronauts Neil Armstrong and Edwin "Buzz" Aldrin set up a moon laboratory with a television camera, scientific equipment and the U.S. flag.

TV camera

U.S. flag

Laser-beam reflector for precise distance measurement

Antenna

Solar power cells

Sensors

They collected 49lbs (22kg) of rock and soil but when the samples were analyzed back on earth there was no evidence of any form of life.

Seismometer to measure for moon quakes

Soil scoop

6

First stage

Second stage

Third stage

Lunar module

Service module

Command module

The Saturn V rocket was designed to take 50 tons of payload (cargo) into lunar orbit. It had three stages and was 364.5 ft (110.6 m) long. It weighed 3,237 tons at launch.

The rocket that took Apollo 11 out of earth's orbit and on to the moon was called the Saturn V. After the third stage the rocket was jettisoned and the command module and the lunar Excursion module made their 238,758 mile (384,400 km) flight to the moon. Astronaut Michael Collins stayed in orbit in the command module while astronauts Buzz Aldrin and Neil Armstrong descended to the moon in the lunar module. When the astronauts had finished their tasks on the moon they returned to the lunar module and blasted up to meet the command module. Once all three astronauts were in the command module again, the lunar module was jettisoned into space and the service module's engines were fired for the return to earth.

UNITED STATES

Lunar module

M2F-1

X24B

X-15A-2

By the time the two astronauts landed on the moon, the Apollo program had cost $22 billion. There were six moon landings in all. Gradually the adventurous, pioneering spirit of the early missions changed to a more practical exploration of space. An example of this is the space shuttle project. It was hoped that developing a reusable space shuttle would cut the cost of placing a pay-load in orbit. But it has so far proved impossible to develop a fully reusable shuttle.

There were several forerunners to the space shuttle. The M2F-1 and the X24B were wingless "lifting bodies" which were dropped from aircraft to test-land on a dry lake bed at Edwards Air Force Base, California. The X-15A-2 rocket-plane had a maximum speed of 4,541 mph (7,311 kph) at altitudes of 325,767 ft (98,816 m). Test craft like these helped scientists find the most suitable shape for the space shuttle.

Building the Shuttle

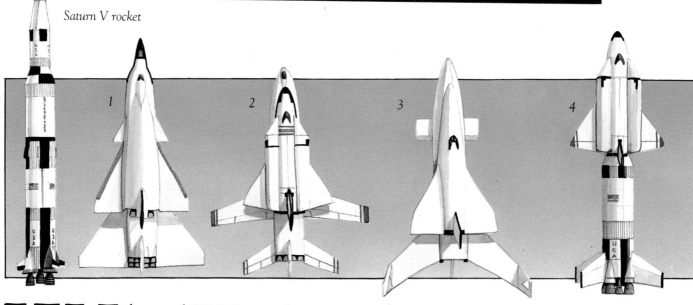

Saturn V rocket

1
2
3
4

With around 600,000 parts, the space shuttle is the most complicated machine ever built. It is the first spacecraft to be reused and since 1981 has had regular flights into space. The idea to make a reusable spacecraft came after the huge launch costs of the Apollo program. There was also the problem of expensive "space garbage" left behind after each mission which could be a danger to future spacecraft. The cost of recovering manned capsules from the ocean when a mission returned was enormous too.

In 1968 NASA began to research the concept of a reusable spacecraft. A great deal was learned from the X-planes program. These experimental aircraft tested the frontiers of aviation in both speed and design. NASA commissioned different companies to come up with a two-stage, fully reusable spacecraft. Many ideas were rejected before the final design of the space shuttle was established.

Early designs for a reusable spacecraft. The first three have "fly back" boosters, which mean they can return to base and land like a plane. Four (above) is a cheaper orbiter mounted on a Saturn 1C rocket.

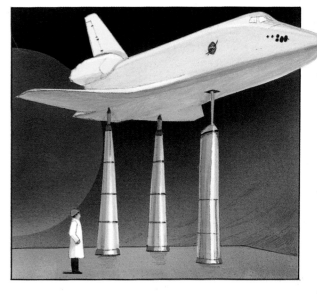

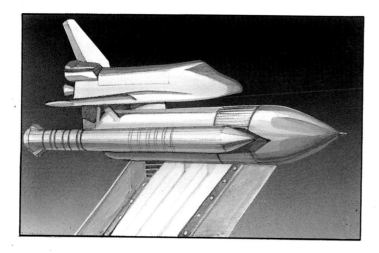

Wind-tunnel tests were vital to the shuttle's design. Above: A one-third scale model was used to test air-flow and its glide capabilities after re-entry. Left: A smaller model, with external tank and boosters, was used to test its aerodynamics at take off.

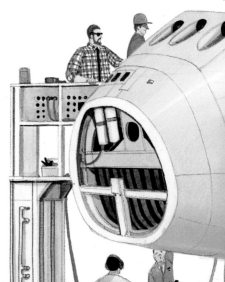

The Enterprise was part of the approach and landing tests, or ALT. The shuttle rode piggyback on a modified Boeing 747-100. This shuttle, which had dummy engines and no external fuel tank, was used to find out how the shuttle glided.

The shuttle is a compromise between a number of designs. The first shuttle was built to test flying and landing in the earth's atmosphere. It was called Enterprise after the spaceship in the *Star Trek* television series. Although this shuttle never flew in space, it acted as a test model for later shuttles. The next shuttle, Columbia, was completed in 1979 at Rockwell International's plant in Palmdale, California, and was the first shuttle to fly in space. Parts were made all over the U.S. and then flown to the Rockwell plant for assembly.

Insulation is vital to stop the shuttle from burning up on re-entry. Reinforced Carbon-carbon (RCC), which can withstand a temperature of $3002°F$ ($1650°C$), is used on the nose and wings' leading edges. Black high-temperature silica tiles are used on the underside, and a combination of insulation blankets and white low-temperature tiles is used elsewhere.

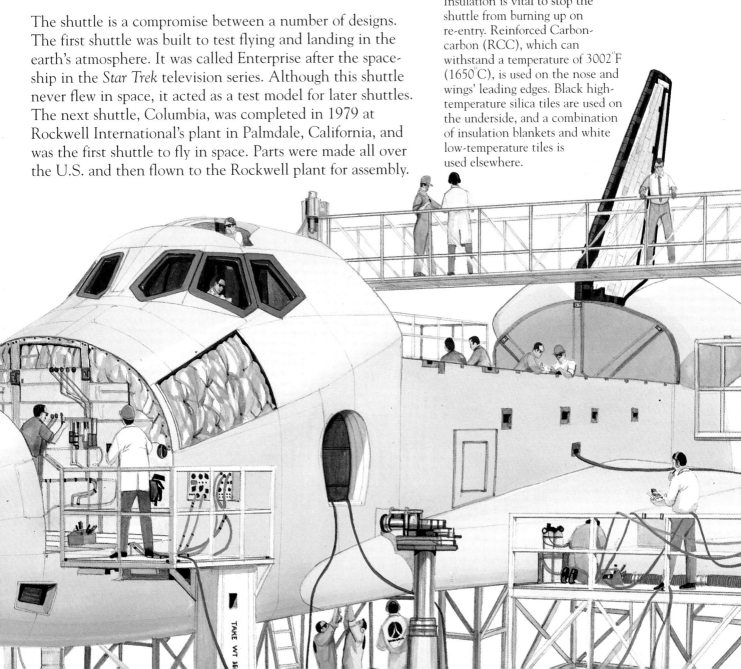

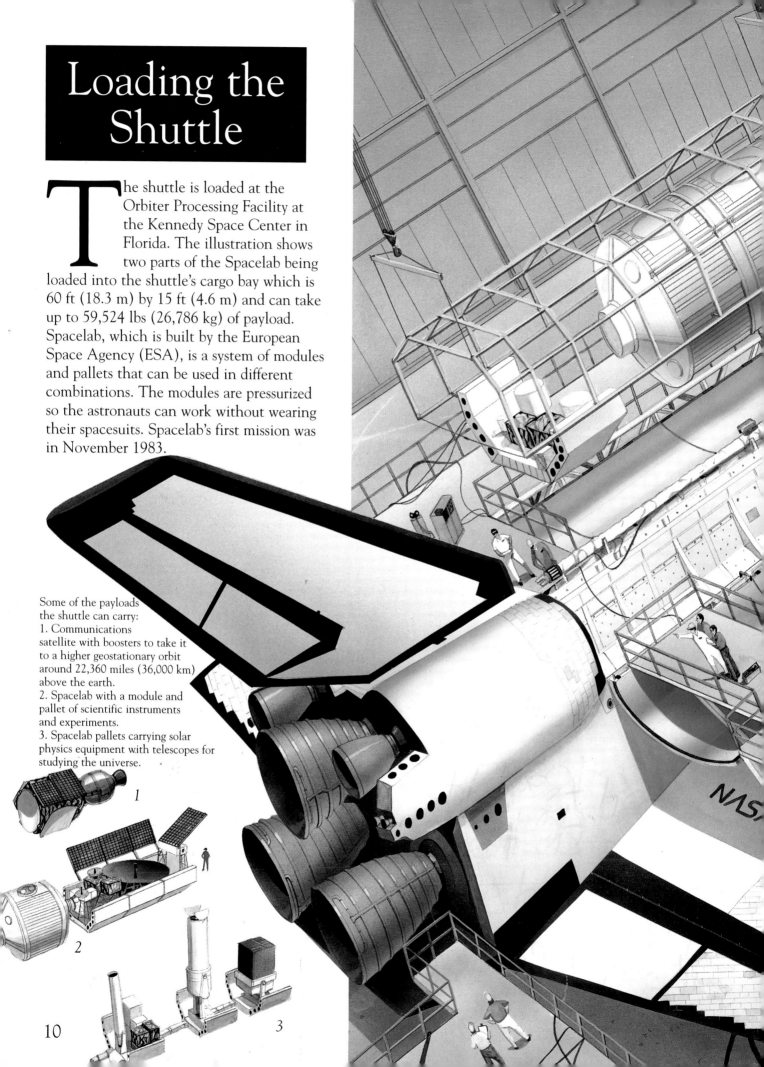

Loading the Shuttle

The shuttle is loaded at the Orbiter Processing Facility at the Kennedy Space Center in Florida. The illustration shows two parts of the Spacelab being loaded into the shuttle's cargo bay which is 60 ft (18.3 m) by 15 ft (4.6 m) and can take up to 59,524 lbs (26,786 kg) of payload. Spacelab, which is built by the European Space Agency (ESA), is a system of modules and pallets that can be used in different combinations. The modules are pressurized so the astronauts can work without wearing their spacesuits. Spacelab's first mission was in November 1983.

Some of the payloads the shuttle can carry:
1. Communications satellite with boosters to take it to a higher geostationary orbit around 22,360 miles (36,000 km) above the earth.
2. Spacelab with a module and pallet of scientific instruments and experiments.
3. Spacelab pallets carrying solar physics equipment with telescopes for studying the universe.

1

2

3

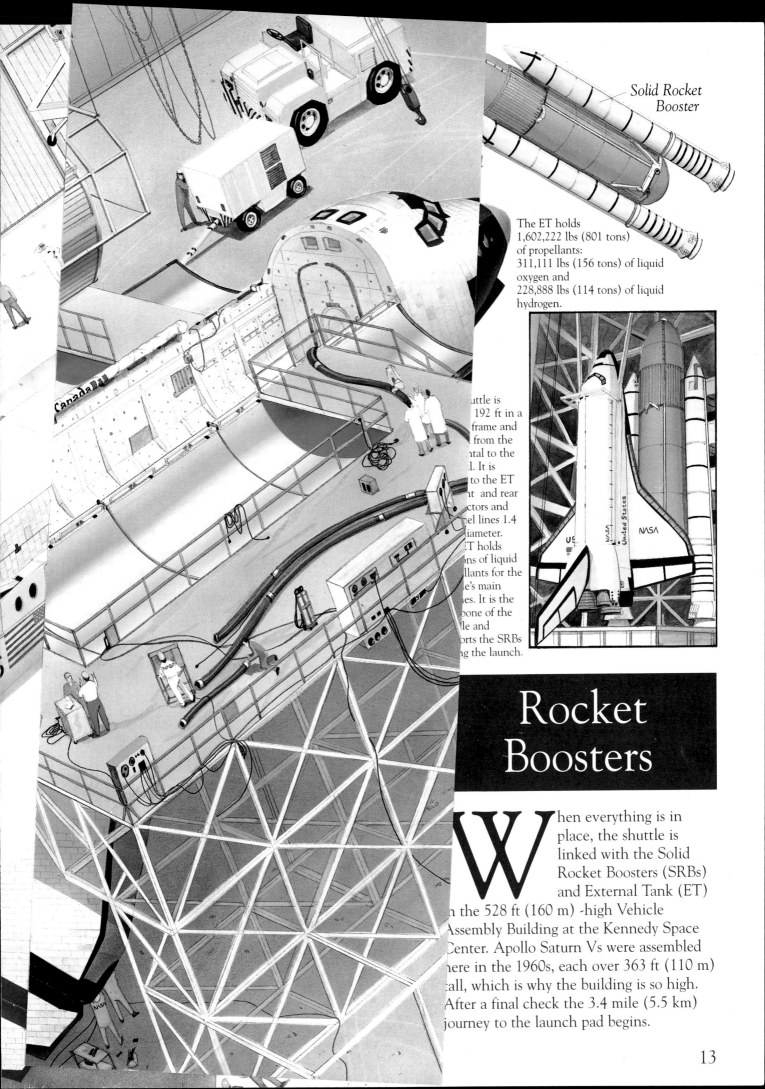

Solid Rocket Booster

The ET holds
1,602,222 lbs (801 tons)
of propellants:
311,111 lbs (156 tons) of liquid
oxygen and
228,888 lbs (114 tons) of liquid
hydrogen.

...uttle is
...192 ft in a
...frame and
...from the
...tal to the
...l. It is
...to the ET
...t and rear
...ctors and
...el lines 1.4
...iameter.
...T holds
...ns of liquid
...llants for the
...e's main
...es. It is the
...pone of the
...le and
...rts the SRBs
...g the launch.

Rocket Boosters

When everything is in place, the shuttle is linked with the Solid Rocket Boosters (SRBs) and External Tank (ET) n the 528 ft (160 m) -high Vehicle Assembly Building at the Kennedy Space Center. Apollo Saturn Vs were assembled here in the 1960s, each over 363 ft (110 m) tall, which is why the building is so high. After a final check the 3.4 mile (5.5 km) journey to the launch pad begins.

The Crawler

The crawler is the biggest tracked vehicle in the world. It is 132 ft (40 m) long and 114 ft (34.7 m) wide and moves on four huge double-tracked crawlers, each one 12 ft (3.7 m) high, 48 ft (14.6 m) long and 2,016 lbs (907 kg) in weight. It was built to carry the Apollo Saturn Vs to the launch pad in the 1960s. When fully loaded with the shuttle and the mobile launch platform, the crawler weighs 17 million lbs (7.7 million kg) and moves at 1 mph (1.6 kph). Unloaded, it can reach 2 mph (3.2 kph).

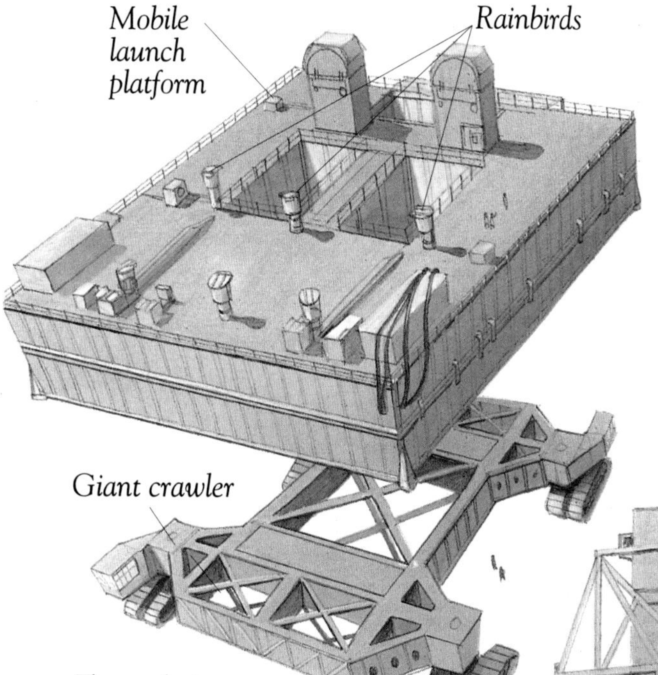

Mobile launch platform

Rainbirds

Giant crawler

The crawler is powered by two 2,750 horsepower diesel engines which guzzle 1.2 gallons (4.5 lt) of fuel for every 23 ft (7 m) the crawler travels.

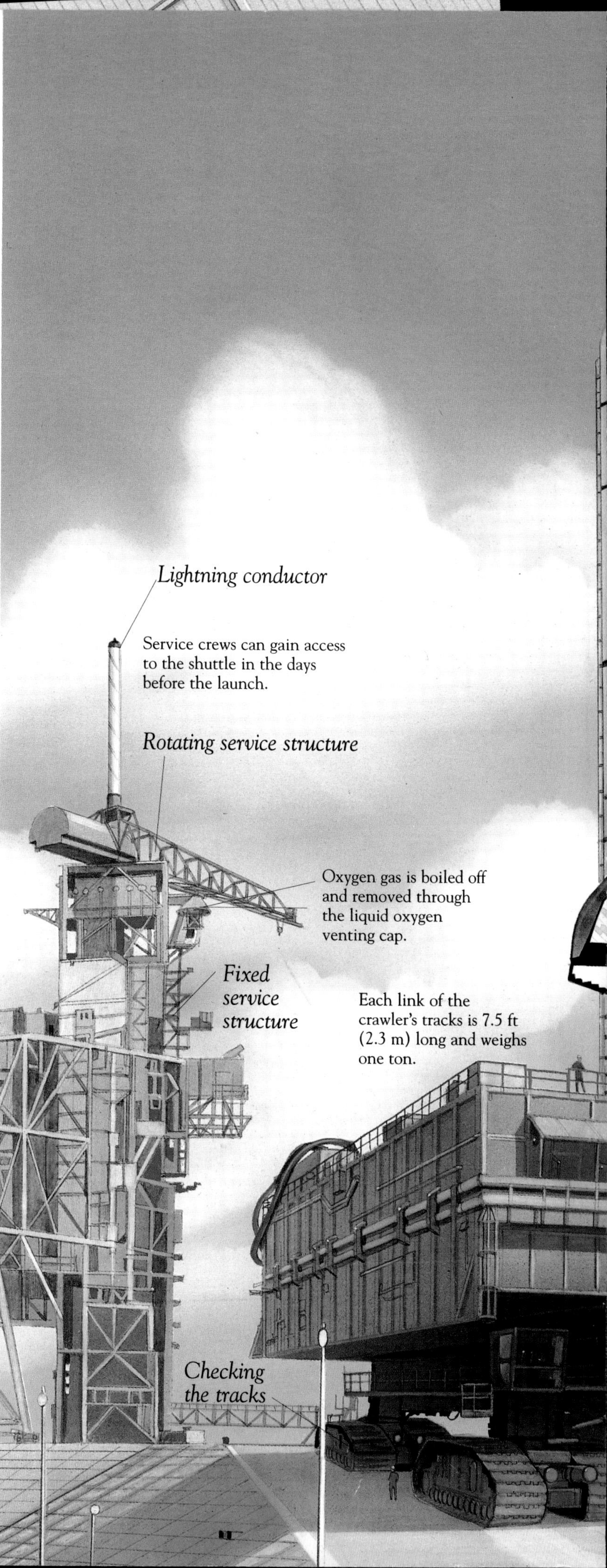

World's most powerful searchlights for security, working and observation

Lightning conductor

Service crews can gain access to the shuttle in the days before the launch.

Rotating service structure

Oxygen gas is boiled off and removed through the liquid oxygen venting cap.

Fixed service structure

Each link of the crawler's tracks is 7.5 ft (2.3 m) long and weighs one ton.

Checking the tracks

Mobile launch platform

Special leveling system keeps crawler exactly level to the ground.

5° incline to launch pad

Lift off!

At first, both the main engines and SRBs help steer the shuttle.

Three minutes before lift off, the Liquid Oxygen Venting Cap (LOVC) on the ET is moved away. At 6.6 seconds the three main engines are ignited and the sound suppression water system is turned on. This pumps over 264,000 gallons (1 million liters) of water onto the launch platform to protect it and the shuttle from the sound of the blast caused by the shuttle's launch – one of the loudest man-made noises.

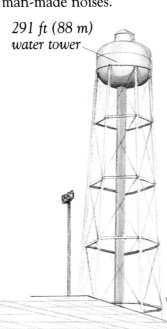

291 ft (88 m) water tower

The launch pad needs protection from the heat of the launch, or else it would be destroyed. Beneath it there is an inverted V-shaped deflector covered with high-temperature concrete which deflects the searing exhaust gases away from the pad.

Propellant storage facility

Two Minutes Later

The SRBs parachute down, landing in the sea about 161 miles (260 km) from the launch site, where they will be picked up by a tug and reused on later missions. The shuttle and ET continue to accelerate upwards. Then, about 8 minutes after lift off, at an altitude of 68 miles (109 km), Main Engine Cut Off (MECO) occurs. The ET, now empty, is jettisoned and will burn up in the atmosphere on re-entry.

Two minutes after lift off and 25 miles (41 km) above the earth, the crew feel a jolt and see a flash of light as the SRBs are pushed away from the ET. Together, the ET and shuttle climb to a higher altitude before the ET, in its turn, is jettisoned. Now the shuttle orbits the earth alone. The altitude of the orbit varies according to the mission with an average of 186 miles (298 km).

At an altitude of 7 miles (11 km) the shuttle is traveling at a speed of around 16,993 mph (27,359 kph). It is guided to the right roll trajectory by the three main engines. The SRBs produce white-hot columns of flame for the first two minutes. When their fuel is finished they are pushed clear by clusters of small rockets.

Just before the launch computers check on the three ignited main engines. If all is well, they permit the SRBs to ignite. Once these are fired the launch cannot be stopped. One minute into the flight the main engines are throttled up to full thrust.

Small rockets propel the SRBs outwards and away from the shuttle.

the launch pad.

18

Space Station

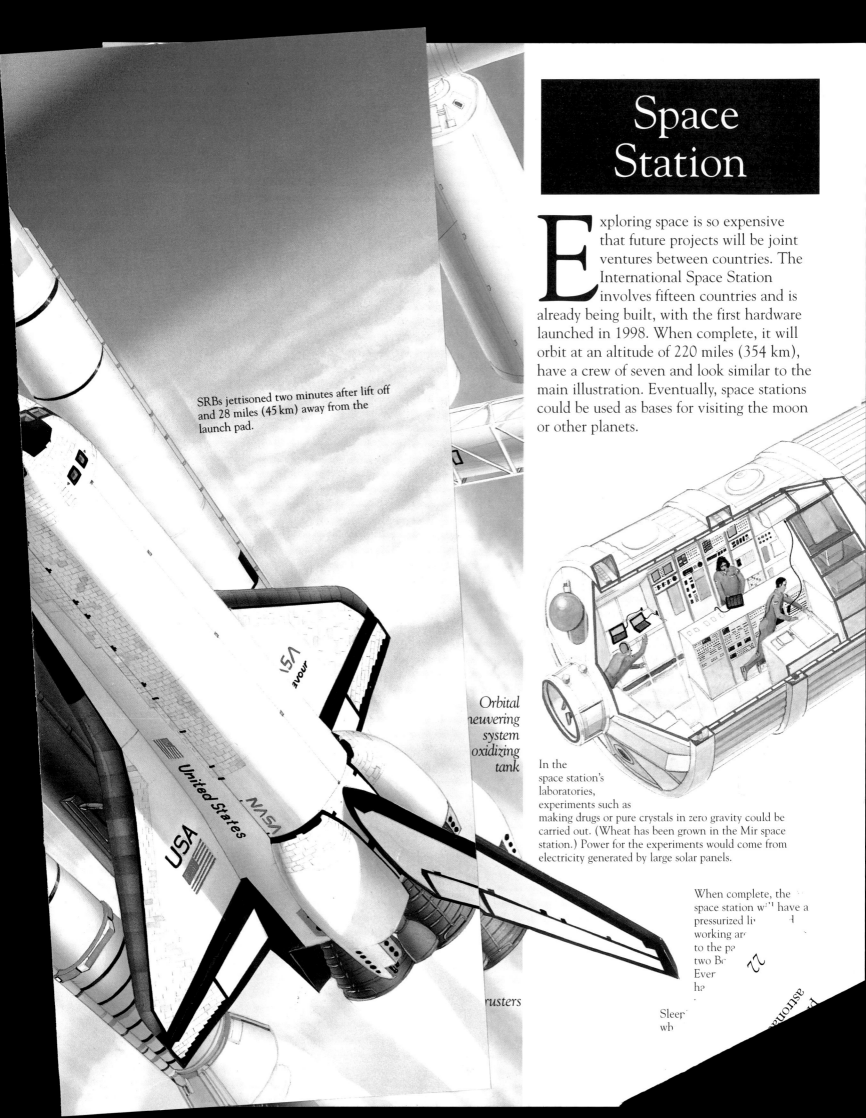

Exploring space is so expensive that future projects will be joint ventures between countries. The International Space Station involves fifteen countries and is already being built, with the first hardware launched in 1998. When complete, it will orbit at an altitude of 220 miles (354 km), have a crew of seven and look similar to the main illustration. Eventually, space stations could be used as bases for visiting the moon or other planets.

SRBs jettisoned two minutes after lift off and 28 miles (45 km) away from the launch pad.

Orbital maneuvering system oxidizing tank

In the space station's laboratories, experiments such as making drugs or pure crystals in zero gravity could be carried out. (Wheat has been grown in the Mir space station.) Power for the experiments would come from electricity generated by large solar panels.

When complete, the space station w'll have a pressurized li⸱
working ar⸱
to the p⸱
two B⸱
Ever
h⸱

Sleep⸱
wh

rusters

22

Living in Space

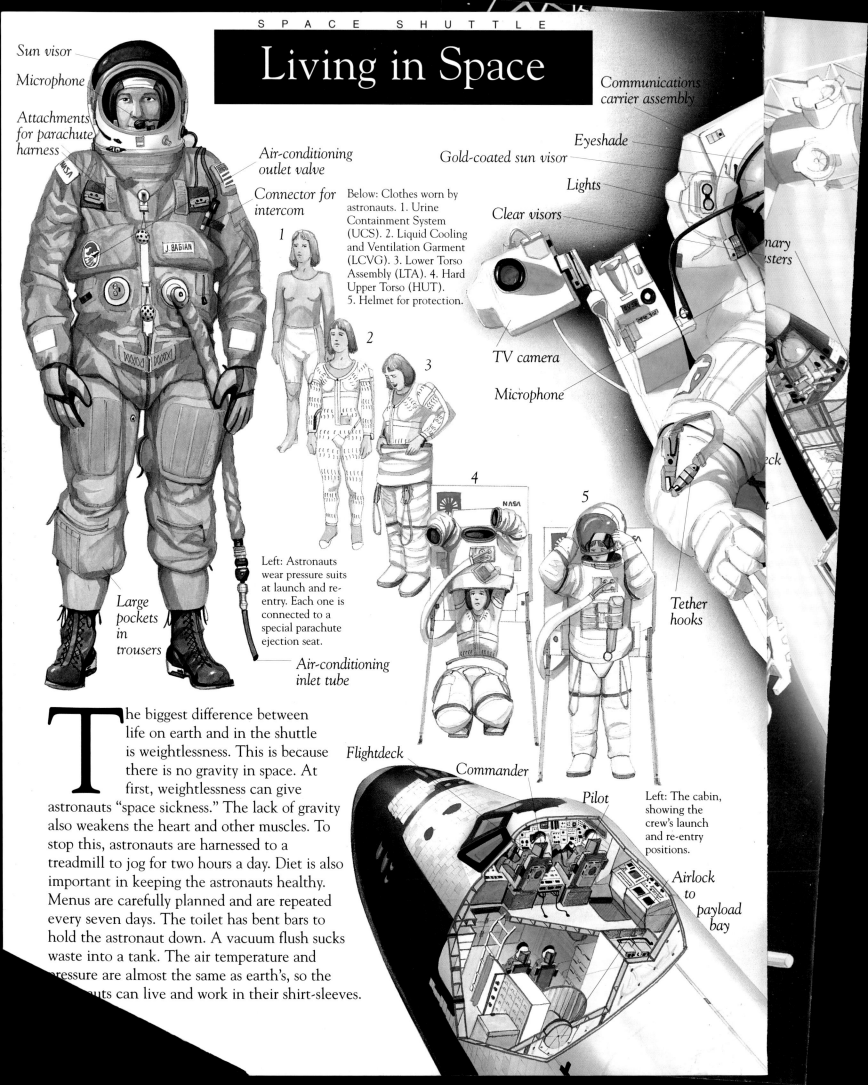

Sun visor

Microphone

Attachments for parachute harness

Air-conditioning outlet valve

Connector for intercom

J.BAGIAN

Large pockets in trousers

Air-conditioning inlet tube

Below: Clothes worn by astronauts. 1. Urine Containment System (UCS). 2. Liquid Cooling and Ventilation Garment (LCVG). 3. Lower Torso Assembly (LTA). 4. Hard Upper Torso (HUT). 5. Helmet for protection.

1

2

3

4

5

NASA

Left: Astronauts wear pressure suits at launch and re-entry. Each one is connected to a special parachute ejection seat.

Communications carrier assembly

Eyeshade

Gold-coated sun visor

Lights

Clear visors

TV camera

Microphone

Tether hooks

Flightdeck

Commander

Pilot

Left: The cabin, showing the crew's launch and re-entry positions.

Airlock to payload bay

The biggest difference between life on earth and in the shuttle is weightlessness. This is because there is no gravity in space. At first, weightlessness can give astronauts "space sickness." The lack of gravity also weakens the heart and other muscles. To stop this, astronauts are harnessed to a treadmill to jog for two hours a day. Diet is also important in keeping the astronauts healthy. Menus are carefully planned and are repeated every seven days. The toilet has bent bars to hold the astronaut down. A vacuum flush sucks waste into a tank. The air temperature and pressure are almost the same as earth's, so the [astron]auts can live and work in their shirt-sleeves.

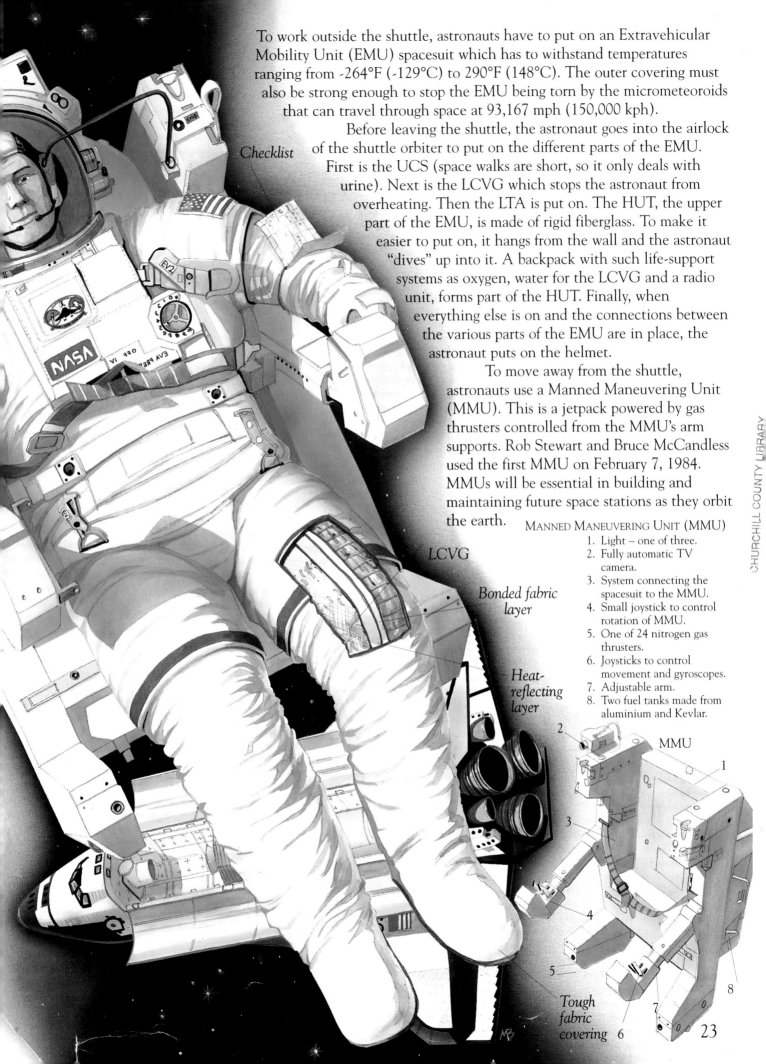

To work outside the shuttle, astronauts have to put on an Extravehicular Mobility Unit (EMU) spacesuit which has to withstand temperatures ranging from -264°F (-129°C) to 290°F (148°C). The outer covering must also be strong enough to stop the EMU being torn by the micrometeoroids that can travel through space at 93,167 mph (150,000 kph).

Before leaving the shuttle, the astronaut goes into the airlock of the shuttle orbiter to put on the different parts of the EMU. First is the UCS (space walks are short, so it only deals with urine). Next is the LCVG which stops the astronaut from overheating. Then the LTA is put on. The HUT, the upper part of the EMU, is made of rigid fiberglass. To make it easier to put on, it hangs from the wall and the astronaut "dives" up into it. A backpack with such life-support systems as oxygen, water for the LCVG and a radio unit, forms part of the HUT. Finally, when everything else is on and the connections between the various parts of the EMU are in place, the astronaut puts on the helmet.

To move away from the shuttle, astronauts use a Manned Maneuvering Unit (MMU). This is a jetpack powered by gas thrusters controlled from the MMU's arm supports. Rob Stewart and Bruce McCandless used the first MMU on February 7, 1984. MMUs will be essential in building and maintaining future space stations as they orbit the earth.

Checklist

LCVG

Bonded fabric layer

Heat-reflecting layer

Tough fabric covering

MANNED MANEUVERING UNIT (MMU)

1. Light – one of three.
2. Fully automatic TV camera.
3. System connecting the spacesuit to the MMU.
4. Small joystick to control rotation of MMU.
5. One of 24 nitrogen gas thrusters.
6. Joysticks to control movement and gyroscopes.
7. Adjustable arm.
8. Two fuel tanks made from aluminium and Kevlar.

MMU

23

Hermes

Columbus space station
docked with Hermes

Hermes and Ariane
rocket

Changing Technology

The Hermes shuttle was developed by the ESA. A small shuttle, 60 ft (18 m) long and with a wingspan of 33 ft (10 m), it would have had a crew of six. However, it was cancelled because of the cost. The free-flying version of the Columbus space station, which Hermes might have supplied, was cancelled for the same reason. But a modular version of Columbus is being developed for the International Space Station.

Below: This design for a Heavy-Lift Launch Vehicle (HLLV) uses the same type of boosters and ET as the present shuttle. It would lift the heavy parts of a space station into orbit on unmanned missions.
Bottom: A space-plane designed by Luigi Colani for Rockwell, makers of the shuttle. It has not yet been built.

N ot only has the shuttle made space travel possible, it has shown governments just how expensive it is. Countries such as the U.S., Russia, and Japan all have space programs, but now there is co-operation in research rather than competition. The long-term goal is to develop a "single stage to orbit" launch vehicle. A vehicle like this would not need booster rockets which have to be jettisoned on the way to space, making space exploration cheaper.

HLLV

Space-plane

Buran

Energia

Left: On November 15, 1987 Energia was test launched by the U.S.S.R. The most powerful booster rocket ever built, it launched the U.S.S.R.'s first space shuttle in 1988. The unmanned test flight flew just two orbits. Although Buran is the U.S.S.R.'s version of the shuttle, it does not have main engines like the shuttle, only orbital maneuvering system engines. Russia has now mothballed the Buran program.

This is the VentureStar Fully Reusable Launch Vehicle (RLV) or X-33. Designed by Lockheed Martin, it is a "single stage to orbit" launch vehicle. It has heat-proof metallic tiles which are tougher and lighter than the present shuttle's silica tiles.

VentureStar

United States
LOCKHEED MARTIN
X-33
Venture Star™

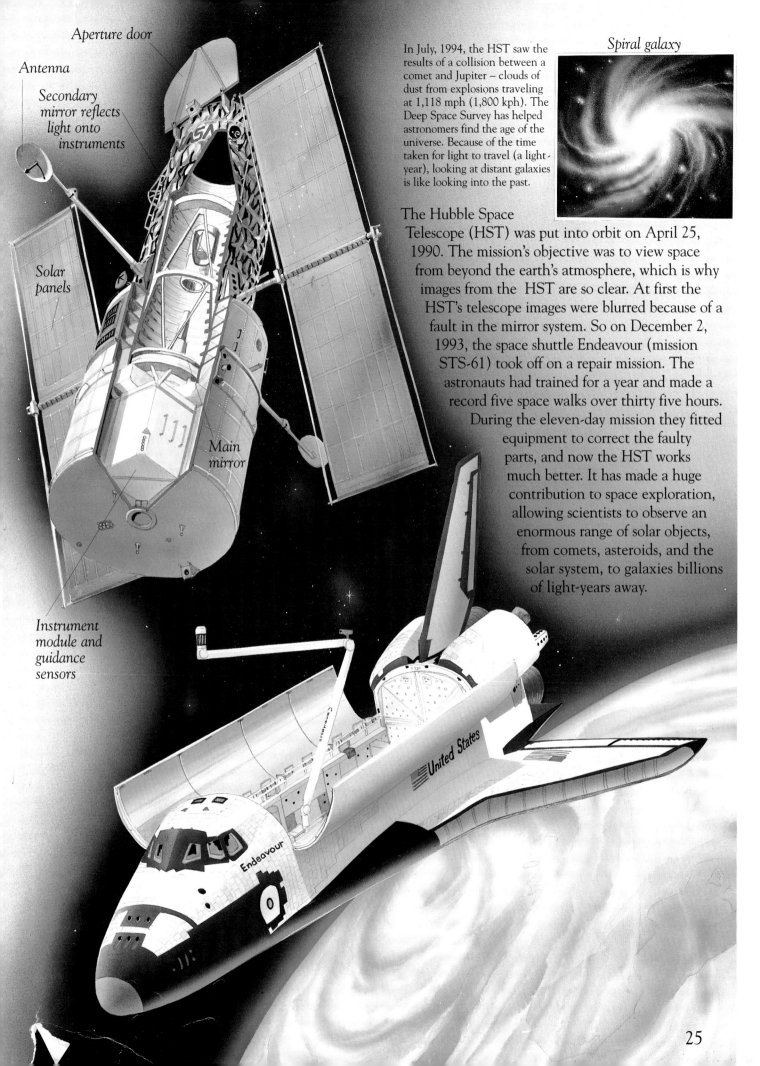

Aperture door

Antenna

Secondary
mirror reflects
light onto
instruments

Solar
panels

Main
mirror

Instrument
module and
guidance
sensors

Spiral galaxy

In July, 1994, the HST saw the
results of a collision between a
comet and Jupiter – clouds of
dust from explosions traveling
at 1,118 mph (1,800 kph). The
Deep Space Survey has helped
astronomers find the age of the
universe. Because of the time
taken for light to travel (a light-
year), looking at distant galaxies
is like looking into the past.

The Hubble Space
Telescope (HST) was put into orbit on April 25,
1990. The mission's objective was to view space
from beyond the earth's atmosphere, which is why
images from the HST are so clear. At first the
HST's telescope images were blurred because of a
fault in the mirror system. So on December 2,
1993, the space shuttle Endeavour (mission
STS-61) took off on a repair mission. The
astronauts had trained for a year and made a
record five space walks over thirty five hours.
During the eleven-day mission they fitted
equipment to correct the faulty
parts, and now the HST works
much better. It has made a huge
contribution to space exploration,
allowing scientists to observe an
enormous range of solar objects,
from comets, asteroids, and the
solar system, to galaxies billions
of light-years away.

United States

Endeavour

Mission specialists control the RMS from the flight deck where they can see both the payload bay and RMS.

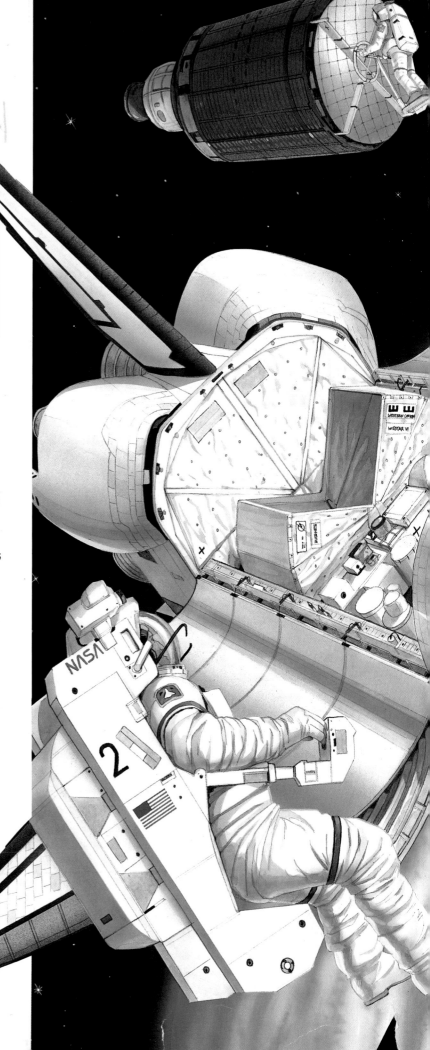

Satellites in Space

Snare device

The RMS is made in Canada.

TV camera

The shuttle normally orbits between 115 miles (185 km) and 258 miles (415 km) above the earth's surface. When it is time to launch a satellite into space, the shuttle's payload bay doors open. Then the satellite is pushed from the bay either by a series of springs or by the Remote Manipulator System (RMS). After it is a safe distance from the shuttle the satellite's rockets fire to put it into a higher geostationary orbit. To retrieve a satellite the shuttle maneuvers to within 39 ft (12 m) of it. Then one of the astronauts uses the RMS to bring it into the payload bay, using a system of cameras and a control stick. Once the satellite is on board, it can be repaired and returned to space or taken back to earth.

The RMS arm is 51 ft (15.32 m) long and has a special wire connector. It can grip, hold and maneuver payloads weighing up to 65,520 lbs or 33 tons (29,484 kg).

Beta cloth covering for thermal protection

Connection to shuttle

Re-entry and Landing

he shuttle is travelling at twenty five times the speed of sound as it re-enters the earth's atmosphere. Then the autopilot makes it take a series of S-turns to slow it down. first turn slows the shuttle by 3,497 mph 30 kph). The thrusters become less ient. The wings and tail control the tilts rolls like a glider. A double sonic boom is d on the ground as the shuttle slows. In last minute it drops 9,624 ft (2,920 m). hough the shuttle can land automatically, mission commander usually takes control t 20 miles (32 km) from the runway n the craft has slowed to 298 mph kph). As the tle touches , parachutes brakes bring it to t 1.5 miles (2.5 km) the runway.

Thermal tiles absorb and radiate the 3,002°F (1650°C) heat of re-entry.

Each tile is glued on by hand and has an identification number.

Heat from the atmosphere causes friction that turns the shuttle's "belly" bright orange.

To reduce drag, wheels are not lowered until the shuttle is only 1,755 ft (532 m) above ground.

The shuttle may land at between 213 and 226 mph (343 and 364 kph), but the astronauts are able to exit by an ordinary set of aircraft steps.

Glossary

Altitude
Height usually above sea level.

Astronaut
Western term for space-pilot.

Atmosphere
The layer of gases, including oxygen, surrounding the earth.

Booster
Shuttle rocket engine which gives a burst of extra power at launch.

Cosmonaut
Term for space-pilot used in Russia and the former USSR.

Geostationary orbit
When a satellite travels at the same speed as the earth and seems to hover over the same spot.

Jettison
To release or throw away.

Lifting body
Wingless aircraft developed to test early space-plane designs.

Light-year
The distance light travels in one year: 5,901 billion miles (9,500 billion km).

Liquid fuel
Fuel that is often in the form of a gas.

Micrometeoroids
The minute particles of dust and rock that litter space.

Mission specialist
An astronaut trained for a special task, e.g. satellite deployment.

Module
Section of a spacecraft.

Orbit
The curved path an object makes as it travels round another object.

Payload
The shuttle's cargo, e.g. a satellite.

Propellant
Substance burned in an engine to produce thrust.

Rainbirds
Nozzles for pouring water on the launch pad to deaden the blast and sound of the shuttle's launch.

Thrust
The pushing force produced by a rocket's engine.

Thruster
Small rocket motor used by a spacecraft or MMU to maneuver.

U.S.S.R.
Union of Soviet Socialist Republics, term by which Russia and its fourteen allied republics were known until Communism collapsed and the republics became independent.

Weightlessness
What astronauts experience in a spacecraft: they float as if they have no weight. That is why they need grab rails to help them move around. Everything else must be fixed in place or it, too, would float around.

Space Shuttle Facts

The shuttle has 34,000 thermal tiles insulating it.

Around 15,000 people help prepare each mission.

Mission control in Houston, Texas, is about 994 miles (1,600 km) from the launch pad at the Kennedy Space Center in Florida.

The air in an EMU is 100% oxygen (on earth it is 20%).

Before leaving the shuttle for space, astronauts must get rid of the nitrogen in their body by breathing pure oxygen for several hours. Otherwise gas bubbles would form in their body fluids. This is "the bends" which deep-sea divers can also suffer.

The payload bay holds 59,524 lbs or 30 tons (26,786 kg).

The shuttle orbits at 5 miles (8 km) per second – over ten times the speed of a rifle bullet!

The shuttle has forty four small thruster engines to maneuver it in space.

On the flight deck there are around 2,100 switches.

The pressure in an EMU stops the astronaut's body fluids boiling.

As the shuttle re-enters earth's atmosphere it is traveling twenty five times faster than the speed of sound.

When an astronaut works in space, the part of the EMU that faces the sun may reach 290°F (148°C). The surface of the side of the suit that faces the darkness of deep space may be -264°F (-129°C).

The RMS is too heavy to work in earth's gravity and can only work in the weightlessness of space.

On a flight of 158 orbits a shuttle can cover a distance of 4,398,668 miles (7,081,855 km).

The whole EMU weighs 107 lbs (48 kg) but takes only a few minutes to put on.

Each shuttle is named after a famous ship: Columbia, Challenger, Discovery, Atlantis and Endeavour.

The shuttle runway at Kennedy Space Center has over 7,996 miles (12,874 km) of grooving cut into it to stop the shuttle hydroplaning (skidding) if it lands after heavy rain.

A shuttle launch takes three and a half days to count down.

Chronology

1232 Chinese use rockets as weapons against Mongol army.

1806 British use rockets against Napoleon's invasion fleet massed at Boulogne.

1865 Jules Verne's novel *From the Earth to the Moon* published.

1903 Konstantin Tsiolkovsky publishes *Exploration of the Universe with Rocket-propelled Devices*, about using rockets for space travel.

1923 German scientist Herman Oberth publishes *The Rocket into Interplanetary Space*, a book on the problems of space flight.

1926 American Robert Goddard launches the first liquid-fueled rocket at Auburn, Massachusetts.

1933 Soviet scientists launch first hybrid solid/liquid fueled rocket. It reaches a height of 1,320 ft (400 m).

1937 German scientists test rockets at Peenemunde on Baltic.

1942 German scientist, Werner von Braun, develops the A-4 rocket which reaches a height of 59 miles (95 km). It is the prototype of V-2 rockets. In 1945 he went to the U.S. and eventually worked on the Apollo space program.

1944 The Germans launch V-2 rockets against London, causing much damage and loss of life.

1949 The U.S.'s two-stage rocket, WAC Corporal, reaches a record height of 250 mi (402 km). Its second stage was a captured V-2 rocket.

1957 U.S.S.R. launches Sputnik 1, the first artificial satellite.

1957 November 3 Sputnik 2 is launched with a dog, Laika, the first animal in space.

1958 January First U.S. satellite, Explorer 1, is launched.

1958 April U.S. forms NASA, the National Aeronautics and Space Administration.

1959 The U.S.S.R. launches Luna 2, the first probe to hit the moon.

1961 April Soviet cosmonaut Yuri Gagarin is the first man in space in Vostok 1.

1961 May Alan Shephard is the first American in space.

1962 February 20 American John Glenn orbits the earth in the Friendship 7 Mercury capsule.

1962 December U.S. Mariner 2 flies past Venus, the first spacecraft to reach another planet.

1963 June The first woman to fly in space is the Russian, Valentina Tereshkova, in Vostok 7.

1964 July U.S. Ranger 7 returns first close-up TV pictures of the moon.

1964 October Three cosmonauts in the U.S.S.R.'s Voshod 1 orbit the earth.

1965 March 18 Alexei Leonor is the first person to walk in space.

1965 July U.S. probe Mariner 4 photographs Mars.

1966 January U.S.S.R. probe Luna 9 lands on the moon.

1967 January Three U.S. Apollo astronauts die in launch-pad fire.

1968 Three U.S. astronauts orbit the moon in Apollo 8.

1969 Apollo astronauts Neil Armstrong and Buzz Aldrin are the first men on the moon.

1971 Capsule from U.S.S.R. probe Mars 3 lands on Mars.

1975 U.S. Apollo spacecraft docks with U.S.S.R.'s Soyuz craft.

1976 U.S. Viking 1 sends photographs from surface of Mars.

1979 U.S. space probe Pioneer 11 flies past Saturn and transmits photographs.

1981 April Launch of first U.S. space shuttle with John Young and Robert Crippen.

1983 June Pioneer is first spacecraft to travel beyond the planets.

1983 November ESA's Spacelab is flown in the shuttle.

1984 April RMS first used to capture a damaged satellite and bring it into Solar Maximum Mission satellite for repair.

1986 January Space shuttle Challenger explodes shortly after launch. Seven crew members die. The U.S. manned space programme is grounded for an investigation.

1986 February Launch of U.S.S.R.'s Mir space station.

1986 March ESA's probe Giotto sends data and photos as it passes Halley's Comet.

1987 May Soviet rocket Energia is launched.

1988 September U.S. resumes manned space program with launch of shuttle Discovery.

1988 November Launch of the U.S.S.R.'s unmanned Buran shuttle.

1989 Voyager 2 encounters Neptune and its moon Triton.

1990 Hubble Space Telescope is deployed by shuttle Discovery.

1994 June Comet Shoemaker-Levy 9 smashes into Saturn's atmosphere. Hubble records result.

1997 June Unmanned spacecraft on supply mission crashes into Mir, causing severe damage. Mir is temporarily out of control.

1997 July Mars Pathfinder probe and Sojourner Rover explore Mars' surface.

Index

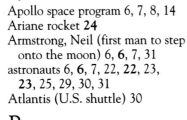